# THE
# AWESOME
# HUMAN
# JOURNAL

## ALSO BY
## NATALY KOGAN

*Happier Now: How to Stop Chasing
Perfection and Embrace Everyday
Moments (Even the Difficult Ones)*

*The Awesome Human Project: Break Free
from Daily Burnout, Struggle Less, and
Thrive More in Work and Life*

# THE AWESOME HUMAN JOURNAL

A Tool Kit for the Tough Days, the Good Days, and All the Days in Between

## NATALY KOGAN

sounds true
BOULDER, COLORADO

Sounds True
Boulder, CO 80306

© 2023 Nataly Kogan

Published 2023

Cover design by Jennifer Miles
Book design by Jennifer Miles and Charli Barnes

Cover image and art by Nataly Kogan

Printed in China

BK06783

ISBN: 978-1-64963-182-4

10 9 8 7 6 5 4 3 2 1

For my Mia and my Avi,
a.k.a. the best life team I could ever ask for.
I love you both beyond.

# INTRODUCTION

Dear Awesome Human,

Being human can be hard.

We all have tough days. There are constant big and small challenges to contend with.

And then there's your brain, which doesn't make dealing with all these challenges any easier. Oh how it loves to trap you in negative thoughts, bring out your inner critic and self-doubter, and make you feel guilty for doing things that bring you joy.

Are you nodding? I'm nodding because my brain is well-trained in doing this, too.

And that's why I created this journal: to help you make the tough days a little better, savor the good days even more, and learn how to create a more supportive relationship with your thoughts and emotions so you can struggle less and thrive more!

Because that's why you're here, on this amazing, unexpected, sometimes difficult life journey: to live fully, savor the good moments (no matter how fleeting they seem at times), and discover your own awesomeness so you can share it with people you care about, in your work, your craft, your community.

You're here to embrace your Awesome Human.

You are **AWESOME** because you have something unique and special to share with this world and so much capacity to be a force of good who positively impacts other humans.

You are **HUMAN** because you don't have unlimited energy, you can't do all things perfectly, and your brain can get in the way with all kinds of unhelpful thoughts.

The only way to fully unleash your awesomeness is by honoring your humanness.

And that's what this journal is all about.

Confession: I might sound confident, but I had to learn this lesson the hard way.

For most of my life, I ignored my humanness, my emotions, and my mental health. I basically treated myself like an accomplishment machine.

I thought life was about always doing more and harder things and struggling through them. So I did that, a lot.

Until several years ago, when I completely burned out and almost lost everything that was meaningful to me.

Figuring out how to recover and heal after my burnout was daunting. I was Googling things like "how to feel better when you feel awful." Like a baby learning to walk and talk, I was learning how to have a more supportive relationship with myself, my thoughts, and my emotions for the very first time.

This is what I call Emotional Fitness: creating a more supportive relationship with yourself, your thoughts, your emotions, and other people.

And throughout this journal, you'll be practicing the **5 Emotional Fitness skills:**

**Acceptance:** Acknowledging the situation and your feelings with clarity vs. judgment, and using that as your starting point to decide the best way forward.

**Gratitude:** Making an active choice to notice the small, positive moments in everyday life—even when times are challenging—and actively expressing your appreciation for other people.

**Self-Care:** Fueling your emotional, mental, and physical energy.

**Intentional Kindness:** Being intentionally kind toward others without expecting anything in return.

**The Bigger Why:** Regularly connecting to your sense of purpose by looking at your daily tasks, projects, and responsibilities through the lens of how they help others, contribute to something bigger than yourself, or help you reach a meaningful long-term goal.

You'll also be learning how to edit your thoughts, treat yourself with compassion, talk back to your brain, say "no" (yes!), and practice your joy (plus a few more skills I'll let you discover as we go).

I handwrote and illustrated this journal—even though I'm not a professional illustrator and my brain threw all possible self-doubt at me—and I want to tell you why:

Every single prompt and practice in this journal I created and tried first myself.

In fact, as I was working on this journal, I looked through many of my own journals where I've jotted down these practices, notes to self, ideas, and words of encouragement for myself.

I'm a science geek—I love understanding how the brain works and then using that understanding to make my brain my friend vs. obstacle creator. And I'll be sharing many Mini Neuroscience Lessons with you throughout this journal because every practice you'll be doing is based on research.

This journal is personal. I'm sharing with you what worked for me and the practices I still use every day to honor my humanness so I can embrace and share my awesomeness. (By the way, it took a lot of practice to quiet my inner critic enough to be able to call myself an Awesome Human, so don't worry if you feel the same way!!)

I've also shared these practices with hundreds of thousands of Awesome Humans through my work and talks and have seen them flourish, savor, and feel more peace within themselves as they practiced (so you don't just have to take my word for it).

OK, I'm going to stop "talking" now because I want you to dive in and begin the beautiful journey of embracing your Awesome Human!

I would love to know how it's going. No, seriously, I would LOVE to see your filled-out practice pages, your Awesome Human Awards, your Notes to Self, and to hear from you directly.

You can always email me at natalyk@happier.com (yes, I read all of the messages, although it takes me a bit of time).

And if you want to inspire other humans to embrace their Awesome Human, share some of your pages on social media and tag @natalykogan and #awesomehuman.

I am rooting for you.

I believe in you.

I am with you, every step of the way.

With love and gratitude,

P.S. This journal is inspired by my book *The Awesome Human Project: Break Free from Daily Burnout, Struggle Less, and Thrive More in Work and Life.* You don't need to read the book to get the most out of this journal, but the book goes deeper into the skills, practices, science, and my personal story. So, I highly recommend getting a copy. Also, I know the author, and she is pretty awesome :)

P.P.S. The art on the cover is a watercolor painting I did called *The Lens of Gratitude.* I began to paint after I burned out as a way to practice my joy, and I fell in love with it. I now share my art in every way I can, including by putting it on the cover of this journal. And I'm telling you this because this is the power of embracing your Awesome Human and practicing your joy: you shine brighter and your joy spreads to so many other people!

Now I'm done talking for real.

Let's dive in!

NOTE TO SELF

Don't do this day
like a chore.

Do it like it's a gift
you're excited to open.

@natalykogan

DAILY PRACTICE PAGES

a brief but

"please-don't-skip-it" tour

# DAILY PRACTICE PAGES INTRO

Small actions and mindset shifts can have a huge impact on how you feel, your outlook, and the way you treat yourself . . . when you practice them consistently.

That's what the Daily Practice pages are for, and you'll find many of them in this journal.

Before I walk you through them, a few quick notes:

- There are two pages of prompts and practices in each set of Daily Practice pages.

- If you can do at least the first page in the morning, awesome. The way you begin your day impacts how you feel during the day, so I'd love for you to give yourself a good start. But make it work for you: if your morning is rushed, do it later! I'd much rather you practice when you can breathe and focus.

- If some of the prompts are a bit more challenging at first, that's OK! Don't judge yourself. You're learning new skills, and the many practices in the journal will help you get better.

OK, now let's take a little tour of the prompts in your Daily Practice pages!

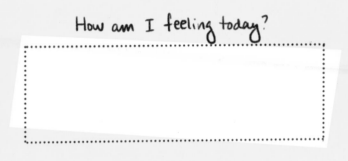

How am I feeling today?

This is your **emotional awareness** practice.

It's a chance to check in with yourself (just like you check in with people you care about).

Write down whatever feelings come up. Simply become aware of them, without judging them.

Based on how you feel, you might think of something you could do to support yourself, but don't force it. Awareness alone is really powerful.

Did you know that emotional awareness leads to improved well-being? It does!

What would I say to a friend who felt this way?

........................................................
........................................................

This is your **self-compassion** practice.

Self-compassion is one of the most important skills of Awesome Humans, and you'll be practicing it a LOT in this journal.

One of the best ways to practice self-compassion is to talk to yourself the way you would talk to a friend.

We tend to be kinder toward our friends than ourselves, and I want to help you change that!

Oh, and self-compassion isn't just for times when you're feeling down! If you're having a great day, celebrate and appreciate yourself!

Self-compassion boosts feelings of self-worth, reduces fear of failure, and increases your overall well-being.

## Today, I'm grateful for...

1 ........................................................
........................................................

2 ........................................................
........................................................

3 ........................................................
........................................................

This is your **gratitude** practice. (If you have time for just one practice on a busy day, this is an awesome choice!)

A couple of tips to make your gratitude practice effective:

- **BE SPECIFIC.** I'm using all caps because this is the most important thing about your gratitude practice. For example, instead of writing "my family," ask yourself *why* you're grateful for your family. The more specific, the better!

- **Smaller = better.** Your brain loves to ignore small, positive moments, but you don't have to let it.

Developing a grateful mindset reduces stress, makes you happier, and fuels your resilience for tough times.

1 thing I could do to have a better day:

This is an opportunity to practice **acceptance,** one of the core Emotional Fitness skills.

Your one thing could be really small! Just the act of deciding to do something to have a better day will fuel you.

Remember that the way you talk to yourself impacts how you feel, so include supportive self-talk on your list of ideas for what you could do.

This prompt is your daily reminder that even when life is challenging, you can always do something to struggle less.

What can I let go of today?

.....................................................................
.....................................................................
.....................................................................

To encourage you to practice and reflect on your Emotional Fitness skills in different ways, you'll find a new question or prompt on each set of your Daily Practice pages.

I have another reason for asking you to answer different questions:

I don't want you to get bored or so used to the daily prompts that you start to glide over them.

If you love one or more of these questions, feel free to make them part of your daily practice!

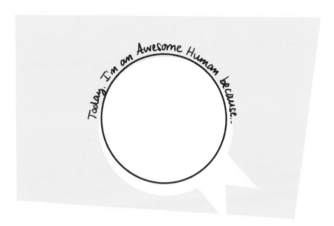

Your inner critic/belittler/doubter has had enough practice. (When I say enough, I mean too much!)

It's time to focus on strengthening your inner appreciator, so every day I'm asking you to complete this sentence:

Today, I'm an Awesome Human because . . .

If you have trouble with it, try this:

Think of someone who cares about you (a friend, significant other, etc.) and, in your mind, ask that person to remind you why you're an Awesome Human.

Having healthy self-esteem improves your relationships with others — so it's never selfish to acknowledge the good in yourself.

OK, that's the tour.

Let's dive in!

→

NOTE TO SELF

You can always

begin again.

@natalykogan

## DAILY PRACTICE

### How am I feeling today?

### What would I say to a friend who felt this way?

### Today, I'm grateful for...

1

2

3

1 thing I could do to have a better day:

What am I looking forward to this week?

Today, I'm an Awesome Human because...

# DAILY PRACTICE

## How am I feeling today?

## What would I say to a friend who felt this way?

## Today, I'm grateful for...

1

2

3

1 thing I could do to have a better day:

What can I let go of today?

..................................................................
..................................................................
..................................................................
..................................................................

Today, I'm an Awesome Human because...

# DAILY PRACTICE

## How am I feeling today?

## What would I say to a friend who felt this way?

## Today, I'm grateful for...

1

2

3

1 thing I could do to have a better day:

How can I be a better friend to myself today?

Today, I'm an Awesome Human because...

NOTE TO SELF

When your day is
over, let it be over.

Don't let its leftovers
ruin the freshness
and possibility of the
next day.

@natalykogan

ANYTIME - YOU - NEED
PRACTICE

## EDIT YOUR THOUGHTS

Your brain thinks about
70,000 thoughts per day (!)
but these thoughts are not
objective facts.

   They are stories — and you
need to edit the thoughts and
stories that cause you to
struggle or stress.

your brain          you

You'll find many MINI NEUROSCIENCE LESSONS in this journal, but to begin, I need to tell you 2 very important things about your brain:

**1:** Your brain's #1 job is to keep you safe from danger

It's always on the lookout for possible danger and has a "negativity bias"— it focuses more on anything negative or what could go wrong because that signals possible danger.

**2:** It makes up a lot of stories based on incomplete information

Your brain can't possibly process all of the stimuli and information in your environment. So it chooses some data points and then makes up stories based on them.

(And because of its negativity bias, the points it chooses and the stories it makes up are often negative.)

So, here's the bad news:

Your thoughts are
not facts.

But understanding this
is AWESOME news, because:

You can EDIT
your thoughts.

# HOW TO EDIT YOUR THOUGHTS

When your brain gives you thoughts that cause you to struggle or get stuck in a negative thought spiral, ask:

## 1. Is this thought true?

For something to be true, it needs to have facts that support it.

## 2. Is this thought helpful?

A helpful thought fuels your energy, motivates you to act, or makes it easier for you to work through a challenge.

# EDIT YOUR THOUGHTS

What thought is causing me to struggle?

> ............................................................
> 
> ............................................................

## Is this thought true?

### FACTS
I know to be true

> ............................
> 
> ............................

### STORIES
my brain has made up

> ....................................
> 
> ....................................

## Is this thought helpful?

☐ Yes          ☐ No

What thought would be more helpful?

> ............................................................
> 
> ............................................................

# Tips for practicing

- Awareness is an important part of this practice. Practice becoming aware of thoughts that cause you to struggle

- A fact is something you can prove. Remember this when you edit your thoughts!

NOTE TO SELF
—"—

You are the

EDITOR

of your

THOUGHTS.

@nataly kogan

Sometimes, your brain gets stuck in a negative thought spiral.

When that happens, you can jump in and interrupt it!

Here are some ideas for how to do it.

MINI NEUROSCIENCE LESSON

When you feel stressed, just the act of deciding to do something to help yourself feel better and then doing that thing helps to lower your stress level.

(What you do turns out to be less important.)

# 3 WAYS TO INTERRUPT A NEGATIVE THOUGHT SPIRAL

## 1

### ZOOM OUT

Think about whether what you're stressed about will matter tomorrow, next week, in a year.

## 2

### TAKE A WALK OUTSIDE

Walking helps to shift your perspective and it releases endorphins, which help you to feel more relaxed.

## 3

### PRACTICE GRATITUDE ANTIDOTE

Acknowledge how you feel and think of 3 specific things you are grateful for. (Gratitude helps to balance out the brain's negativity bias)

Try it ➜

# GRATITUDE ANTIDOTE

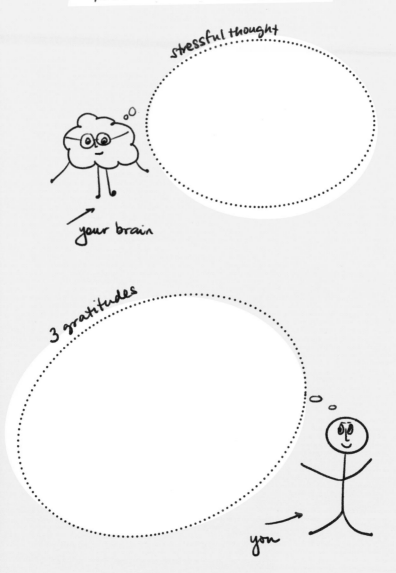

stessful thought

your brain

3 gratitudes

you

Introducing...

Awesome Human Awards

It's not easy to practice your Awesome Human skills (and your brain can be very stubborn).

So you absolutely deserve to get awards when you succeed at practicing them!

· You get to decide when to award these to yourself (aka Awesome Human honor code)

· Have fun! Color them, add scented stickers or glitter... (glitter is awesome, obviously)

P.S. Show off your awards! Share them on social media and tag @natalykogan and #awesomehuman

# AWESOME HUMAN

### Awarded to:

........................................
*your name*

for successfully editing

unhelpful thoughts

(even if it was just

1 thought)

## AWARD

........................................
*date awarded*

## DAILY PRACTICE

How am I feeling today?

What would I say to a friend who
felt this way?

Today, I'm grateful for...

1

2

3

1 thing I could do to have a better day:

.................................................................
.................................................................

How was I kind this week?

.................................................................
.................................................................
.................................................................
.................................................................

Today, I'm an Awesome Human because...

## DAILY PRACTICE

How am I feeling today?

What would I say to a friend who felt this way?

Today, I'm grateful for...

1

2

3

1 thing I could do to have a better day:

What imperfection could I practice accepting in myself?

Today, I'm an Awesome Human because...

Take a...

CREATIVITY
BREAK!

## Welcome to your first creativity break!

If your brain just said something silly about how you are not creative, you don't have to listen.

To be human is to be creative.

Creativity is seeing something through your unique personal lens and then expressing that feeling, idea, or vision in some way.

There are roughly a bajillion reasons why making time for creativity is essential to thriving and embracing your Awesome Human, but I added CREATIVITY BREAKS to this journal for a whole other reason:

It feels AWESOME to do something creative!

So have fun and I hope you come up with many of your own CREATIVITY BREAKS!

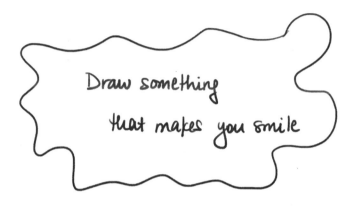

Draw something that makes you smile

Sunflowers?

Ice cream cones?

Balloons?

The ocean?

Flowers?

Anything goes and there are

NO RULES!

# MY SMILE DRAWING

## MINI NEUROSCIENCE LESSON

Doing something creative
releases dopamine, a
chemical that contributes
to feeling good.

Creativity reduces stress
and helps you to process
challenging emotions.

What are some creative
activities you want to do
more often or explore?

(shhh, this is now your awesome
"creative stuff to have fun with"
list — come back here
for ideas when you need one!)

# DAILY PRACTICE

### How am I feeling today?

### What would I say to a friend who felt this way?

### Today, I'm grateful for...

1

2

3

1 thing I could do to have a better day:

What has felt meaningful to me recently?

Today, I'm an Awesome Human because...

# DAILY PRACTICE

## How am I feeling today?

## What would I say to a friend who felt this way?

........................................................

........................................................

## Today, I'm grateful for...

1 ....................................................

....................................................

2 ....................................................

....................................................

3 ....................................................

....................................................

1 thing I could do to have a better day:

.......................................................................

How can I practice my joy today?

.......................................................................
.......................................................................
.......................................................................
.......................................................................

Today, I'm an Awesome Human because...

NOTE TO SELF

You can't give
what you don't have.

@natalykogan

Woohoo! It's time
for your

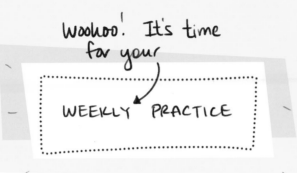

::::::::::::::::::::::::::::::::::::::::
WEEKLY  PRACTICE
::::::::::::::::::::::::::::::::::::::::

## SELF-CARE CHECK-IN

... because you are
an Awesome Human and
not superhuman and you
need to fuel your energy
to do all the Awesome Human
things you want to do

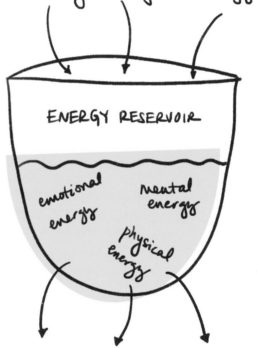

SELF-CARE =

intentionally fuel your energy

ENERGY RESERVOIR

emotional energy

mental energy

physical energy

... and do less of what unnecessarily drains it

**Self-care is the skill of fueling your energy.**

You are a human being and every single thing you do requires energy.

Think about a car: It needs fuel — gasoline or electricity — to do its job of being a car.

You never treat fuel as a luxury because you know that the car can't function without it.

**Your energy is your fuel and it's essential for you to function.**

This is what self-care is all about and I want to help you make it a priority and practice it consistently.

A weekly SELF-CARE CHECK-IN is an awesome way to do it. Try it now.

→

What has been fueling my energy?

How could I do this more?

your
energy reservoir

What has been draining my energy?

How could I do this less?

## Tips for practicing...

- **Pick a day.** Doing your check-ins on the same day each week will help you to stay consistent.

- **Be specific.** The more specific you can be with your answers, the more effective your SELF-CARE CHECK-INs will be.

- **Be realistic.** Small shifts and actions that you do consistently have a huge impact.

- **Commit to you.** Treat your self-care commitments as promises you make to yourself.

NOTE TO SELF

Exhaustion
is not
a badge of honor.

@natalykogan

Awesome
Human

Acts of
Kindness

It feels so good to do something
kind for another person, doesn't it?

But life gets busy, you get stressed
out, and sometimes, kindness falls
off your priority list.

That's why Intentional Kindness is
one of the core skills of Awesome
Humans ⌐

↳ when you treat it
as something you regularly
practice, you make it
important and don't
leave it to chance.

You'll find a few Awesome Human Acts of Kindness practices in this journal, but I'd love for you to brainstorm and <u>DO</u>! a few of your own, too!

How about now?

NOTE TO SELF

The greatest joy
in life is to bring
joy to someone else.

@natalykogan

# ACTS OF KINDNESS BRAINSTORM

what small acts of
kindness could you do?

pick 1 and do it today!

## MINI NEUROSCIENCE LESSON

........................................

When you do something kind,
your brain releases oxytocin,
which makes you feel good,
and serotonin, which helps
to regulate your mood.

Practicing kindness also helps
you to feel less alone and
more connected to others,
which is essential for well-being
and mental health.

# DAILY PRACTICE

## How am I feeling today?

## What would I say to a friend who felt this way?

## Today, I'm grateful for...

1
2
3

1 thing I could do to have a better day:

........................................................

........................................................

How could I let my best qualities
be in charge today?

........................................................
........................................................
........................................................
........................................................

Today, I'm an Awesome Human because...

How am I feeling today?

What would I say to a friend who felt this way?

Today, I'm grateful for...

1

2

3

1 thing I could do to have a better day:

What energy do I want to bring
to my interactions with others this week?

.....................................................................
.....................................................................
.....................................................................
.....................................................................

Today, I'm an Awesome Human because...

As you've seen, I wrote you
many NOTES-TO-SELF in this
journal — and I would love
for you to get into the habit
of writing them to yourself.

- It could be something
  you want to remember

- Perhaps a few words of
  encouragement

- An intention for the day

Think of your NOTES-TO-SELF
as something a good friend would
write to you — and practice being
that friend to yourself!

# WRITE A NOTE-TO-SELF

**NOTE TO SELF**

Share your NOTE-TO-SELF on social media!

Tag @natalykogan
#awesomehuman

It would bring me immense joy to see it and you would inspire others, too.

## DAILY PRACTICE

### How am I feeling today?

### What would I say to a friend who felt this way?

### Today, I'm grateful for...

1

2

3

1 thing I could do to have a better day:

What is something I can't control
that I could accept?

...........................................................................
...........................................................................
...........................................................................
...........................................................................

Today, I'm an Awesome Human because...

NOTE TO SELF

Being human
     is hard.

Don't expect yourself
to do it perfectly.

@natalykogan

## TALK TO YOURSELF
## LIKE A FRIEND

Unfortunately, most of us are too familiar with the harsh inner critic who lives in our brain.

But you can learn to quiet your inner critic by practicing self-compassion (aka treating yourself as you would a friend).

you →

← also you, as a friend

# SELF-COMPASSION 101

Self-compassion means:

☑ You acknowledge that you are a human being

☑ Like all human beings, you can't do everything perfectly and sometimes you make mistakes (omg!)

☑ When something goes wrong or you make a mistake or fail at something, you treat yourself in a way that reduces struggle

... like you would treat a friend!

One of the most powerful ways to practice self-compassion is to practice talking to yourself as you would to a friend.

TRY IT!

# TALK TO YOURSELF LIKE A FRIEND

## Unkind self-talk

"You are so lazy — you didn't finish what you planned to do!"

## What you'd say to a friend

"You probably overestimated what you could get done. Get some rest and start fresh tomorrow."

# Tips for practicing.

- Pick a friend and imagine that you're talking to him or her as you practice.

- Don't become discouraged if this is challenging at first. If your inner critic has been allowed to talk to you non-stop for years, it will take time for your voice of self-compassion to become more confident.

- Remember: Any progress is still progress!

    (This is a good reminder for _all_ practices.)

# AWESOME HUMAN

Awarded to:

............................

your name

for not allowing your
inner critic to run free
and talking to yourself
like a friend

## AWARD

............................

date awarded

## NOTE TO SELF

Self-acceptance
doesn't mean that
you never improve.

It means you improve
from a place of love
and self-respect.

@natalykogan

Because I know from personal experience – and working with so many Awesome Humans – just how stubborn our inner critic can be, I've created a bonus practice that I would love for you to try (and then practice, practice, practice – did I mention that this takes practice?).

I call it GRATITUDE EXCHANGE

check it out!

## GRATITUDE EXCHANGE

Every time your inner critic
speaks up, reply with
something you appreciate
about yourself.

## WHY IT WORKS

Your brain's negativity bias
also applies to how you see
yourself. So your inner critic
gets a lot of airtime (it loves to
focus on "what's wrong") and
your inner appreciator stays quiet
(and doesn't tell you about
so much that is good and
awesome about you!).

GRATITUDE EXCHANGE trains
your inner appreciator to
speak up.

your inner appreciator

# Practice your GRATITUDE EXCHANGE!

things my inner critic says

things my inner appreciator says

# AWESOME HUMAN SELF-TALK

5 things to say to yourself daily
6

| | |
|---|---|
| You are enough | You can always begin again |
| I believe in you | You deserve your own kindness |
| You are an Awesome Human! | |

Add your own!

When you practice positive self-talk,
use "you" or your name vs. "I."

This helps to make it more effective
— like a good friend talking to you.

## MINI NEUROSCIENCE LESSON

The way you talk to yourself
significantly impacts how
you feel and your ability
to work through challenges.

Positive self-talk increases
motivation and resilience.

Negative self-talk increases
stress and anxiety.

# DAILY PRACTICE

How am I feeling today?

What would I say to a friend who felt this way?

........................................................

........................................................

Today, I'm grateful for...

1 ........................................................

........................................................

2 ........................................................

........................................................

3 ........................................................

........................................................

1 thing I could do to have a better day:

My intention for this week is:

Today, I'm an Awesome Human because...

# DAILY PRACTICE

### How am I feeling today?

### What would I say to a friend who felt this way?

................................................................

................................................................

### Today, I'm grateful for...

1 ............................................................

   ............................................................

2 ............................................................

   ............................................................

3 ............................................................

   ............................................................

1 thing I could do to have a better day:

......................................................................................

What tiny promise do I want to make to myself today?

......................................................................................
......................................................................................
......................................................................................
......................................................................................

Today, I'm an Awesome Human because...

83

Write a gratitude note
to one of your "imperfections"

Pick something about you that
your inner critic loves to criticize.

A body part, a habit, anything.

Think about why you might be
grateful to this "imperfection."

Look at this "imperfection" with kind
   eyes as if it were valuable and
                              loved.

      And now, write a gratitude
      note to your "imperfection."

Dear ......................................,
"imperfection"

I haven't told you lately (or ever),
but I'm grateful for you because:

......................................
......................................
......................................
......................................
......................................
......................................

And while I know that I can be unkind
to you, in the future I will try to:

......................................
......................................
......................................
......................................
......................................
......................................

With love,

......................................
your signature

# DAILY PRACTICE

## How am I feeling today?

## What would I say to a friend who felt this way?

## Today, I'm grateful for...

1

2

3

1 thing I could do to have a better day:

How could I practice more intentional kindness today?

........................................................

........................................................

........................................................

........................................................

Today, I'm an Awesome Human because...

How am I feeling today?

What would I say to a friend who felt this way?

Today, I'm grateful for...

1

2

3

1 thing I could do to have a better day:

How did I make myself proud
this week?

........................................................
........................................................
........................................................
........................................................

Today, I'm an Awesome Human because...

## NOTE TO SELF

Setting boundaries
is not about saying "no."
It's about saying "YES"
to what is most
important to you.

@natalykogan

## HONOR YOUR BOUNDARIES
### (aka say "no")

Saying "no" is hard. You're afraid to disappoint people or worry that they will be angry with you.

But deep down, you know that you need to set boundaries to protect your well-being — and this means learning how to say "no" sometimes.

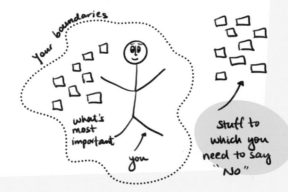

your boundaries

what's most important

you

stuff to which you need to say "NO"

Here are questions to ask
yourself before making a
commitment (big or small)

☐ Can I energetically
afford to do this?

☐ If I commit to doing this,
what do I have to do <u>less</u>
or <u>not do</u> to make sure
I have enough energy?

☐ Am I saying "YES" out of
fear or because doing this
is important to me?

☐ Would "tomorrow me" feel
awesome about my making
this commitment today?

## NO/YES TRADEOFF

I need to say (NO) to:

........................................................
........................................................
........................................................

So I can say (YES) to:

........................................................
........................................................
........................................................

(NO) may be to specific tasks, commitments, or requests for help, but it could also be to your inner perfectionist who wants you to do what you know will drain you

(YES) may be to specific tasks or commitments, but it could also be to how you want to feel and show up for people in your life

## Tips for practicing

- The YES/NO TRADEOFF is an awesome practice to use when you realize that you can't energetically afford to say "yes" to something but your brain tries to make you feel guilty about saying "no".

- When you worry about how someone might react to your "no" think about how you would react — and give the other person some credit.

NOTE TO SELF

People who love you
will never want you
to do something out
of obligation or fear.

@natalykogan

AWESOME HUMAN

Awarded to:

................................

your name

for honoring what's most

important to you

by saying "no" to

what isn't.

AWARD

................................

date awarded

# WEEKLY PRACTICE: SELF-CARE CHECK-IN

What has been fueling my energy?

> ........................................................

How could I do this more?

> ........................................................

your energy reservoir

What has been draining my energy?

> ........................................................

How could I do this less?

> ........................................................

# DAILY PRACTICE

## How am I feeling today?

## What would I say to a friend who felt this way?

## Today, I'm grateful for...

1 ..................................................
   ..................................................

2 ..................................................
   ..................................................

3 ..................................................
   ..................................................

1 thing I could do to have a better day:

What advice would my future self give me today?

........................................................
........................................................
........................................................
........................................................

Today, I'm an Awesome Human because...

# DAILY PRACTICE

## How am I feeling today?

## What would I say to a friend who felt this way?

## Today, I'm grateful for...

1

2

3

1 thing I could do to have a better day:

How do I want to impact others this week?

.........................................................
.........................................................
.........................................................
.........................................................

Today, I'm an Awesome Human because...

# DAILY PRACTICE

## How am I feeling today?

## What would I say to a friend who felt this way?

....................................................

....................................................

## Today, I'm grateful for...

1 ...............................................

...............................................

2 ...............................................

...............................................

3 ...............................................

...............................................

1 thing I could do to have a better day:

How could I approach this day
with more enthusiasm?

........................................................
........................................................
........................................................
........................................................

Today, I'm an Awesome Human because...

NOTE TO SELF

Challenge is constant.

Struggle is optional.

@natalykogan

## GET OUT OF THE
## VALLEY OF STRUGGLE

The Valley of Struggle is the distance between how something is and how your brain decided it should be.

We all get stuck in it from time to time — and it can really drain our energy.

But you can learn how to get out of it.

The best way to get out of
the VALLEY OF STRUGGLE is to use
the LENS OF ACCEPTANCE.

**Step 1**  Look at the situation — and
your feelings — with <u>clarity</u> vs.
<u>judgment</u>

| Clarity | Judgment |
|---|---|
| Facts you know to be true | Your brain's opinion about the facts |
| (e.g. it's raining on our vacation) | (e.g., it shouldn't be raining on our vacation!) |

⊕ <u>Acknowledge</u> how you feel
(e.g. annoyed that it's raining!)

**Step 2**  Given the facts and how you
feel, identify 1 step you <u>could</u>
take to move forward with less struggle

(e.g. we could find something fun
to do inside until the rain stops)

# LENS OF ACCEPTANCE

## Your Valley of Struggle

---

**Step 1**  Look at the situation and your feelings with clarity (vs. judgment)

| Facts | Judgment |
|-------|----------|
|       |          |

### How do you feel?

---

**Step 2**  What is 1 thing you could do to move forward with less struggle?

---

## Tips for practicing

- "Should" is shorthand for being stuck in the VALLEY OF STRUGGLE.

- Use your Editing Your Thoughts skills to make sure you don't mistake your brain's stories for facts.

- Often, there is nothing you can do about the situation you are in. But there is always 1 step you could take to help yourself struggle less.

### For example, you could:

- acknowledge and accept how you feel without judgment

- choose to focus your attention on something you can control

- treat yourself with compassion and care

## NOTE TO SELF

Acceptance has nothing to do with resignation.

It's about seeing reality clearly so you can move forward in the best way.

@natalykogan

# AWESOME HUMAN

Awarded to:

..............................................

Your name

for successfully climbing out
of the Valley of Struggle
(even if it took a while)

# AWARD

..............................................

date awarded

Appreciating yourself and taking care of your needs leads to improved mental health, greater resilience, and reduced stress and anxiety.

OK, I can't let you turn the page
without reminding you to

TURN THE LENS OF ACCEPTANCE
TOWARD YOURSELF !!!

Yes, I am shouting because we
cause ourselves so much struggle
by "shoulding" ourselves!

How does all this "shoulding"
yourself make you feel?

I immediately feel resistance, like
I'm starting from behind, failing
at it before I even begin.

But using the Lens of Acceptance
you can shift from "should" to "could."

SHOULD = resistance

COULD = possibility

TRY IT!

(I gave you a few
examples to get you started)

## I SHOULD

"I should spend
less time on my
phone."

"I should be
further along in
my career."

## I COULD

"I could put my
phone away
after 9 pm."

"I could take a
leadership class
this year."

One day, when I was stuck
  in the VALLEY OF STRUGGLE,
I made a quick checklist to
 help me get out of it.

   It helped, and I still use it
    — so, of course, I want
    to share it with you.

NOTE TO SELF
—"—

You are not here

to struggle through life.

You are here

to __thrive!__

@natalykogan

# VALLEY OF STRUGGLE CHECKLIST

☐ Is the way I'm thinking about this causing me to struggle more?

☐ Is this fueling or draining?

☐ Is this thought helpful?

☐ Am I treating myself as I would treat a friend?

☐ What is 1 step I could take to move forward with less struggle?

☐ ........................................
........................................
........................................

↗

Do you want to add something that helps you get out of frustration or unhelpful thought loops? Do it!

# DAILY PRACTICE

### How am I feeling today?

### What would I say to a friend who felt this way?

### Today, I'm grateful for...

1 ...............................................................
...............................................................

2 ...............................................................
...............................................................

3 ...............................................................
...............................................................

1 thing I could do to have a better day:

How could I do less of what
drains my energy today?

............................................................
............................................................
............................................................
............................................................

Today, I'm an Awesome Human because...

# DAILY PRACTICE

## How am I feeling today?

## What would I say to a friend who felt this way?

........................................................

........................................................

## Today, I'm grateful for...

1 ....................................................

....................................................

2 ....................................................

....................................................

3 ....................................................

....................................................

1 thing I could do to have a better day:

My favorite moments of joy this week:

Today, I'm an Awesome Human because...

## NOTE TO SELF

Relaxing is <u>not</u>
         doing nothing.

It's the practice of loosening
the grips of stress, tension,
and overdoing that we
all accumulate.

It's productive and essential.

@natalykogan

# WEEKLY PRACTICE: SELF-CARE CHECK-IN

What has been fueling my energy?

┌─────────────────────────────────────┐
│                                     │
│                                     │
│                                     │
└─────────────────────────────────────┘

How could I do this more?

┌─────────────────────────────────────┐
│                                     │
│                                     │
│                                     │
└─────────────────────────────────────┘

your energy reservoir

What has been draining my energy?

┌─────────────────────────────────────┐
│                                     │
│                                     │
│                                     │
└─────────────────────────────────────┘

How could I do this less?

┌─────────────────────────────────────┐
│                                     │
│                                     │
│                                     │
└─────────────────────────────────────┘

## Awesome Human Acts of Kindness

Awesome
Human

Acts of
Kindness

Give someone an
AWESOME HUMAN
AWARD!

Use the next page to create
an AWESOME HUMAN AWARD for
someone in your life.

→

Think of a friend, family member,
or colleague you appreciate
and tell them why.

Have fun creating the
award! Use markers or
pencils to color it!

Cut it out to give it to its recipient
or take a photo to send it
electronically.

AWESOME HUMAN

...............................
name

You are an Awesome Human
because:

AWARD

## NOTE TO SELF

Gratitude

is the shortest path

to joy.

@natalykogan

I want to encourage you
to do more small acts
of kindness, so here's
something AWESOME!

- Take a photo of the
Awesome Human Award
you create

   (bonus points if
   the recipient is
   in the photo!)

- Share it on social media
and tag @natalykogan

- I will send you an
Awesome Human surprise!

## DAILY PRACTICE

### How am I feeling today?

### What would I say to a friend who felt this way?

### Today, I'm grateful for...

1

2

3

1 thing I could do to have a better day:

What unhelpful thought isn't serving me (and I could let go)?

Today, I'm an Awesome Human because...

# DAILY PRACTICE

## How am I feeling today?

## What would I say to a friend who felt this way?

## Today, I'm grateful for...

1

2

3

1 thing I could do to have a better day:

Given how things are, what is this day inviting me to do?

........................................................
........................................................
........................................................
........................................................

Today, I'm an Awesome Human because...

# WEEKLY PRACTICE: SELF-CARE CHECK-IN

What has been fueling my energy?

How could I do this more?

your energy reservoir

What has been draining my energy?

How could I do this less?

Every time you see something **YELLOW** today, say something encouraging to yourself!

## Why yellow?

- ✓ I love yellow and it's one of my favorite colors
- ✓ Yellow boosts your mood
- ✓ It's bright and distinctive

Feel free to repeat this challenge as often as you'd like!

# DAILY PRACTICE

How am I feeling today?

What would I say to a friend who felt this way?

......................................................
......................................................

Today, I'm grateful for...

1 ......................................................
......................................................

2 ......................................................
......................................................

3 ......................................................
......................................................

1 thing I could do to have a better day:

What does self-acceptance
mean to me?

.................................................
.................................................
.................................................
.................................................

Today, I'm an Awesome Human because...

## DAILY PRACTICE

How am I feeling today?

What would I say to a friend who felt this way?

..............................................................................
..............................................................................

Today, I'm grateful for...

1 ...........................................................................
...........................................................................

2 ...........................................................................
...........................................................................

3 ...........................................................................
...........................................................................

1 thing I could do to have a better day:

::::::::::::::::::::::::::::::::::::::::::::::::::::
:                                                :
:                                                :
:                                                :
::::::::::::::::::::::::::::::::::::::::::::::::::::

How do I get to help or contribute
this week?

.................................................
.................................................
.................................................
.................................................

Today, I'm an Awesome Human because...

# DAILY PRACTICE

## How am I feeling today?

## What would I say to a friend who felt this way?

........................................................................
........................................................................

## Today, I'm grateful for...

1 ....................................................................
........................................................................

2 ....................................................................
........................................................................

3 ....................................................................
........................................................................

1 thing I could do to have a better day:

What would my younger self be
proud of me for?

......................................................
......................................................
......................................................
......................................................

Today, I'm an Awesome Human because...

NOTE TO SELF

You see what
you look for.

So look for beauty,
goodness, kindness,
hope.

@natalykogan

## CHOOSE YOUR
## MENTAL LENS

Our brains have many "default" lenses. For example, you already know about the negativity bias lens — the brain's tendency to focus more on the negative.

But this is where you come in:

You GET TO CHOOSE THE LENS through which you see your day, your life, your work, yourself, people in your life...

... and the lens you choose has a huge impact on how you feel and the choices you make.

mental lens

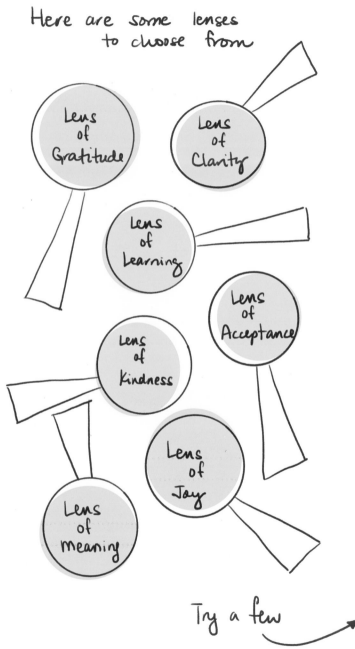

Here are some lenses
to choose from

Lens of Gratitude

Lens of Clarity

Lens of Learning

Lens of Acceptance

Lens of Kindness

Lens of Joy

Lens of Meaning

Try a few

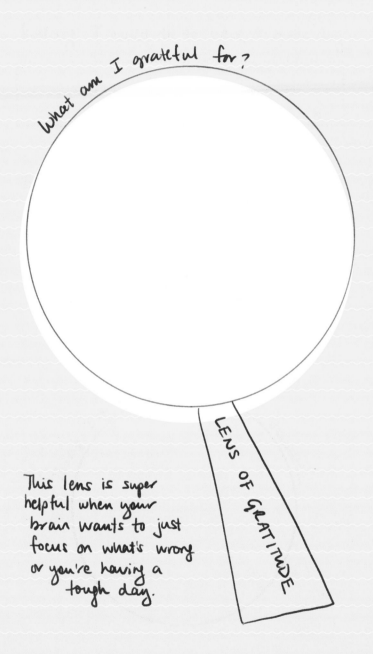

What am I grateful for?

LENS OF GRATITUDE

This lens is super helpful when your brain wants to just focus on what's wrong or you're having a tough day.

How does what I'm doing help others?

LENS OF MEANING
(aka Bigger Why)

This lens can help you reframe tasks you need to do (and maybe don't feel like doing) and fuel your motivation to get them done.

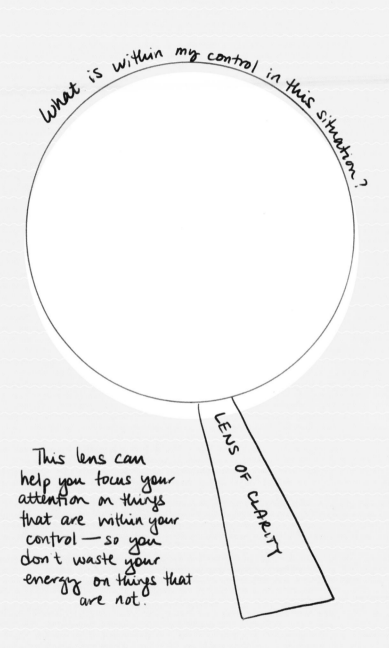

What is within my control in this situation?

LENS OF CLARITY

This lens can help you focus your attention on things that are within your control — so you don't waste your energy on things that are not.

How could I find more joy in this day?

LENS OF JOY

If you find yourself just going through the motions, this is a great lens to help you infuse more joy in your day.

- If you get stuck in a loop of unhelpful thoughts or are having a rough day, ask:

"What lens might help me struggle less right now?"

- Feel free to make up your own lenses - of course!

- Remember that your brain has many default lenses so if you're frustrated or stressed about a situation, practice becoming aware of the default lens through which your brain is seeing it - and then choose one that serves you better.

145

AWESOME HUMAN

Awarded to:

......................................

your name

for choosing to look at

a difficult situation

through the Lens of

......................................

(fill in)

AWARD

......................................

date awarded

# WRITE A NOTE-TO-SELF

## NOTE TO SELF

Share your NOTE-TO-SELF on social media!

Tag @natalykogan
# awesomehuman

## AWESOME HUMAN CHALLENGE

**Take a 10-minute fuel-up break**

✓ get away from your screens

✓ take a walk outside
(inside is OK, too)

✓ do something that
feels refreshing

Bonus (that's not actually a bonus):

DO THIS AT LEAST
ONCE A DAY and put
it on your calendar!

If your brain tells you that
   you can't possibly take a break,
and you have too much to do,
   you can just read this out loud
         (a few times!).

## MINI NEUROSCIENCE LESSON

When you take a break, the
default mode network in
your brain is extremely
active. This network is
responsible for essential
activities, like processing and
organizing information, integrating
memories, finding solutions
to problems, and generating
         creative ideas.

## DAILY PRACTICE

How am I feeling today?

What would I say to a friend who felt this way?

.........................................................
.........................................................

Today, I'm grateful for...

1 ......................................................
.........................................................

2 ......................................................
.........................................................

3 ......................................................
.........................................................

1 thing I could do to have a better day:

........................................................
:                                                      :
:                                                      :
:                                                      :
:                                                      :
........................................................

Words I want to say to myself
more often:

....................................................
....................................................
....................................................
....................................................

Today, I'm an Awesome Human because...

# DAILY PRACTICE

## How am I feeling today?

## What would I say to a friend who felt this way?

## Today, I'm grateful for...

1

2

3

1 thing I could do to have a better day:

What tiny act of kindness could I do today?

...........................................................

...........................................................

...........................................................

...........................................................

Today, I'm an Awesome Human because...

## CREATIVITY BREAK!

Draw your portrait
through the eyes of someone
who loves you

## THE RULES:

1. Don't panic!

2. Think of someone who loves you and reflect on what they love about you.

3. Imagine you're that person and draw yourself through their eyes.

4. Your drawing doesn't have to look like you! It could be a flower, a shape, or something completely abstract.

5. Have fun!

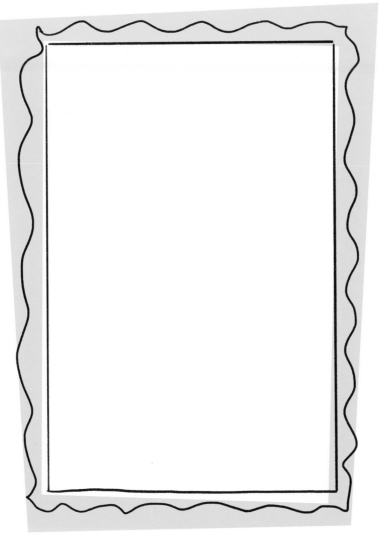

My portrait through
the eyes of:

..........................................

## DAILY PRACTICE

How am I feeling today?

What would I say to a friend who felt this way?

............................................................

............................................................

Today, I'm grateful for...

1 ............................................................

............................................................

2 ............................................................

............................................................

3 ............................................................

............................................................

1 thing I could do to have a better day:

This week, I value how I:

.............................................................
.............................................................
.............................................................
.............................................................

Today, I'm an Awesome Human because...

How am I feeling today?

What would I say to a friend who felt this way?

Today, I'm grateful for...

1

2

3

1 thing I could do to have a better day:

What piece of advice do I need
to hear today?

..................................................
..................................................
..................................................
..................................................

Today, I'm an Awesome Human because...

## NOTE TO SELF

Spend more time
talking to your brain
than listening to it.

@natalykogan

## TALK BACK TO YOUR BRAIN

Fear is at the root of so many unhelpful thoughts we experience:

- Self-doubt is your brain on fear of failure.

- Worrying about how others may judge you is your brain on fear of not belonging.

But instead of listening to these fear-based thoughts, you can TALK BACK TO YOUR BRAIN!

# How to TALK BACK TO YOUR BRAIN
## when it gives you fear-based thoughts

### Step 1: Get honest about the fear

Is your brain afraid of:
- how others might judge you?
- something going wrong?
- how you will feel?

### Step 2: Talk back to your brain!

- Acknowledge the fear
- Remind your brain why this thought is not helpful
- Redirect its attention to something specific that <u>would be helpful</u>

Give it a try!

# TALK BACK TO YOUR BRAIN

your brain's
fear-based
thought

Fear of :

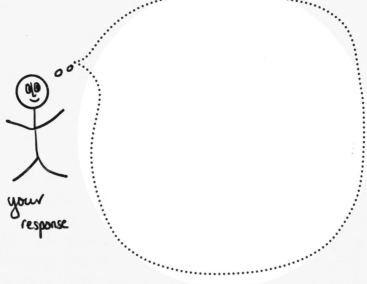

your
response

## Tips for practicing

- Be honest with yourself about what's causing your brain to feel fear — this helps to move forward.

- The more specific you can be about the thought you want your brain to focus on, the better.

### MINI NEUROSCIENCE LESSON

Fear is the brain's natural response when you're facing uncertainty, doing something new or challenging.

Acknowledging the fear helps you to move through it with less struggle.

# AWESOME HUMAN

## Awarded to:

........................................
your name

for impolitely and courageously
talking back to your brain
when it gave you thoughts
rooted in fear

## AWARD

........................................
date awarded

**Awesome Human**

**Acts of Kindness**

Leave a compliment for a stranger

Think of a compliment you would like to receive and write it down on the next page.

Cut it out and give the note to someone you encounter today — or snap a photo and email or text it to a friend or colleague!

You could also leave this compliment note for someone to find (in a coffee shop, for example).

Come back to do this again! (and you can always use sticky notes, too)

# COMPLIMENT NOTES

# awesome human

# awesome human

# awesome human

You deserve your own
kindness.

Everything you need
is already within you.

Don't forget to be proud
of yourself.

# WEEKLY PRACTICE: SELF-CARE CHECK-IN

What has been fueling my energy?

How could I do this more?

your
energy reservoir

What has been draining my energy?

How could I do this less?

# DAILY PRACTICE

## How am I feeling today?

## What would I say to a friend who felt this way?

## Today, I'm grateful for...

1

2

3

1 thing I could do to have a better day:

What quality do I admire in myself?

..................................................
..................................................
..................................................
..................................................

Today, I'm an Awesome Human because...

# DAILY PRACTICE

How am I feeling today?

What would I say to a friend who felt this way?

Today, I'm grateful for...

1

2

3

1 thing I could do to have a better day:

If this day was a gift, what would the gift be?

Today, I'm an Awesome Human because...

# DAILY PRACTICE

## How am I feeling today?

## What would I say to a friend who felt this way?

........................................................
........................................................

## Today, I'm grateful for...

**1** ...................................................
........................................................

**2** ...................................................
........................................................

**3** ...................................................
........................................................

1 thing I could do to have a better day:

................................................................

A moment recently when I felt
true to myself:

................................................................
................................................................
................................................................
................................................................

Today, I'm an Awesome Human because...

NOTE TO SELF

Your joy
is never frivolous.

It's your

LIFE FUEL.

@natalykogan

## PRACTICE YOUR JOY

Has your brain told you that doing something that brings you joy is selfish or a waste of time or money?

Probably. I always wanted to paint but my brain told me that it was useless and unproductive.

But your joy can never be useless! It fuels your being, your energy, and your motivation, and it helps you to share your awesomeness with others.

177

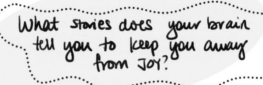

What stories does your brain tell you to keep you away from Joy?

I don't deserve to feel joy because...

.......................................................................
.......................................................................
.......................................................................

The things that bring me joy are too...

.......................................................................
.......................................................................
.......................................................................

(expensive, frivolous, etc.)

I can't feel joy until...

.......................................................................
.......................................................................
.......................................................................

(everyone else is happy, I lose weight, I make more money, etc.)

Awareness is so powerful.

Often, just becoming aware of our unhelpful stories helps us to break through them.

But here's a question I want you to ask yourself if your brain is being stubborn:

DOES BELIEVING THIS STORY HELP YOU LIVE THE LIFE YOU WANT TO LIVE?

We both know the answer is a very loud <u>NO!</u>

It's time to write a NEW JOY STORY!

# MY NEW JOY STORY

Joy is my life fuel.

When I practice my joy, I feel...

....................................................
....................................................
....................................................

Practicing my joy positively impacts the
people I care about because...

....................................................
....................................................
....................................................

I will no longer deny myself joy because...

....................................................
....................................................
....................................................

Joy is my Awesome Human fuel!

# PRACTICE YOUR JOY

Schedule some time every week for your JOY PRACTICE!

Even 20-30 minutes is awesome and yes, please put it on your calendar so you take it seriously.

Jot down a few ideas for your JOY PRACTICE right now!

Tips for practicing:

· Try new things! Use your joy practice as an opportunity to explore new hobbies without any pressure to be good at them.

· If your brain tries to guilt you or tells you that focusing on your joy is selfish, here's some good material to use when you TALK BACK TO YOUR BRAIN!

MINI NEUROSCIENCE LESSON

Human emotions are contagious.

When you have a friend who is happier, you're 25% more likely to be happier.

You can spread joy to other people.

AWESOME HUMAN

Awarded to:

..............................
your name

for practicing your JOY

without guilt

(because it's your

life fuel)

AWARD

..............................
date awarded

# DAILY PRACTICE

## How am I feeling today?

## What would I say to a friend who felt this way?

## Today, I'm grateful for...

1

2

3

1 thing I could do to have a better day:

How could I cultivate a more
supportive relationship with myself?

..................................................................
..................................................................
..................................................................
..................................................................

Today, I'm an Awesome Human because...

## DAILY PRACTICE

How am I feeling today?

What would I say to a friend who felt this way?

Today, I'm grateful for...

1

2

3

1 thing I could do to have a better day:

What have I done recently that felt invigorating and fueling?

Today, I'm an Awesome Human because...

## CREATIVITY BREAK!

Draw a
secret drawing

## THE RULES:

1. Give yourself 10 mins to draw anything you want.

2. Do **NOT** show this drawing to anyone. <u>Ever.</u>

3. Keep this drawing secret even from your inner critic.

(This is a great way to explore your creativity — feel free to do other secret creative projects!)

# MY SECRET DRAWING

## DAILY PRACTICE

### How am I feeling today?

### What would I say to a friend who felt this way?

### Today, I'm grateful for...

1

2

3

1 thing I could do to have a better day:

My favorite thing my brain tells me:

...............................................................
...............................................................
...............................................................
...............................................................

Today, I'm an Awesome Human because...

## DAILY PRACTICE

### How am I feeling today?

### What would I say to a friend who felt this way?

### Today, I'm grateful for...

1

2

3

1 thing I could do to have a better day:

........................................................
........................................................
........................................................

How could I prioritize feeling
more peaceful today?

........................................................
........................................................
........................................................
........................................................

Today, I'm an Awesome Human because...

193

What has been fueling my energy?

How could I do this more?

your energy reservoir

What has been draining my energy?

How could I do this less?

## AWESOME HUMAN

Awarded to:

........................................
your name

for recognizing that you
can't give what you don't have
and making self-care
a priority

AWARD

........................................
date awarded

# WRITE A NOTE-TO-SELF

NOTE TO SELF

Share your NOTE-TO-SELF on social media!

Tag @natalykogan
# awesome human

# THE AWESOME HUMAN SOS TOOL KIT

(for those tough life moments when you need some extra help or a nudge in the right direction)

you →

worry

burnout

overwhelm

self-doubt

# QUICK INTRODUCTION
# TO YOUR SOS TOOL KIT

Dear Awesome Human,

Sometimes, even if you're super diligent about practicing your emotional fitness skills, you get stuck.

I practice them a LOT and teach them to thousands of other people, and this still happens to me.

My self-doubt gets overwhelming.

Or I worry too much about the future or a situation I can't control.

This happens to all of us. It's part of being human.

And that's why I created this section: to help you through those times when you get stuck, overwhelmed, or burned out.

When you feel that way, first, remember to treat yourself with compassion, like you would a friend. (This means yelling at yourself for getting stuck is out of the question.)

Then, turn to this section and find a practice that resonates, one that feels like it could guide you or offer some relief.

WORRIED ABOUT
THE FUTURE
(and all the things
that could go wrong)

## MINI NEUROSCIENCE LESSON

Uncertainty is extremely challenging for the human brain to handle.

When we face uncertainty, the brain releases cortisol, the stress hormone, as a way to prepare us to fight or flee from possible danger.

Why do we spend so much time
worrying about the future?

If you remember that your brain's
#1 priority is to keep you safe from
danger, you can probably guess:

The future is uncertain
so your brain worries
about possible danger.

So here's a surprisingly effective
technique to reduce nonstop worrying:

Think through the worst-case
scenario to give your brain
some comfort that if it happens,
you will be OK.

The next time you get stuck
in a worry loop, try this

## MEET THE WORST-CASE SCENARIO

What's the worst-case scenario that could happen?

How would you feel if this happened?

What steps would you take to move forward?

Who could you ask for help or support?

Do you think you could get through this scenario and be OK?

☐ Yes  ☐ No

NOTE TO SELF
Your brain loves
to focus on what's
wrong.
Remind it about
what could go right.
@natalykogan

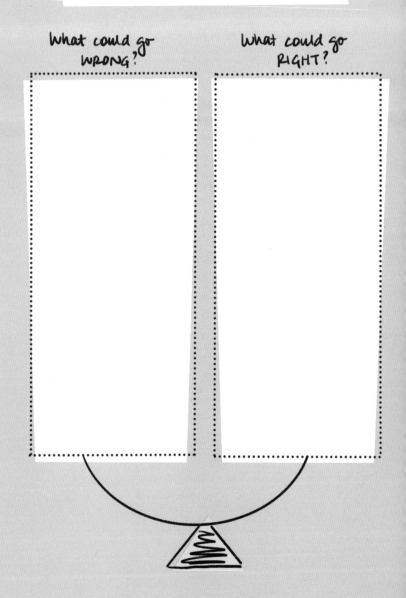

NEGATIVITY BIAS BALANCER

What could go WRONG?

What could go RIGHT?

This is a great opportunity to practice TALKING BACK TO YOUR BRAIN!

Let's think about all the things that could go wrong!

your brain's negativity bias

I know you're afraid of what might happen because things are uncertain. But this constant worry is only stressing me out. Instead, let's think about all the things that could go right:

..............................................
..............................................
..............................................
..............................................
..............................................

your response

NOTE TO SELF

Getting untired
takes time.

@natalykogan

FEELING

BURNED OUT

(or drained or just

really tired)

I want to say something to you
that I wish I had heard a few years
ago when I was burned out
and trying "to get back to normal"
as fast as possible:

There is no hack or shortcut
to healing from burnout.

There is only one path:

YOU HAVE TO MAKE
YOUR WELL-BEING YOUR
#1 PRIORITY.

Yes, this means that some other
things will need to come off
your to-do list. You may need
to say "no" a lot. But this is
the only way forward.

There are 2 parts to your

**REFUEL AND RECHARGE MINI PLAN**

**Part 1**

Create ⟦3 Daily Anchors⟧ that
will help to fuel your energy

your

energy
reservoir

**Part 2**

Identify 3 energy drains
and take specific steps to reduce them.

Let's start with Part 2
(because in my experience,
we tend to forget how
important this is).

Put a ☑ next to the things
that drain your energy and
add any others below:

~~~~~~~~~~~~~~~~~~~~~~~~~~~~~~~~~~

☐ too much screen time

☐ not taking breaks

☐ negative self-talk

☐ worrying about the future/
    uncertainty

☐ trying to do everything perfectly

☐ ........................................................

☐ ........................................................

☐ ........................................................


Pick ③ energy drains that are
within your control and ⟶

... come up with specific, realistic ways to reduce them

| Energy drain | How I will reduce it |
|---|---|
| e.g., too much screen time | Put away my phone at 9 pm every night |
| ① | |
| ② | |
| ③ | |

(the more specific you can be about your action steps, the better!)

If your brain tells you that
there are too many energy drains
you can't control, TALK BACK TO
YOUR BRAIN and remind it:

✓ to practice the LENS OF ACCEPTANCE
and focus on what you <u>could do</u>
given how things are

✓ that yes, you may need to get
some help (from your boss,
colleagues, family members, friends...)

NOTE TO SELF
——— '' ———

Asking for help
is not a sign of weakness.

It is a testament
to your humanity.

@natalykogan

Reminder:  Many of the practices in this journal can help you reduce your energy drains.

- If your inner critic is relentless, practice TALKING TO YOURSELF LIKE A FRIEND (p. 69)

- If you're working nonstop, without breaks, add a daily MINI FUEL-UP (p. 148)

- If you are having trouble saying "no," practice the NO/YES TRADEOFF (p. 93)

Now, your mission is to come up with 3 Daily Anchors to FUEL your energy.

Creating Daily Anchors — and sticking to them — helped me feel more calm, centered, and able to deal with all the things, so I could heal from burnout.

So let's come up with yours!

First, jot down some things that fuel your energy (don't forget to include some that bring you joy!).

Here are some ideas for your
Daily Anchors — put a √
next to any you want to try.

~~~~~~~~~~~~~~~~~~~~~~~~~~~~

☐ a walk or run outside

☐ yoga / meditation / quiet time

☐ reading time

☐ going to bed on time

☐ doing something creative

☐ sitting down to eat a meal
without rushing

## MY 3 DAILY ANCHORS

Pick 3 energy fuels and make a commitment to do them every day (aka most days!)

.....................................................................

I commit to supporting myself daily by practicing my
### 3 DAILY ANCHORS:

1. ...........................................................
   ...........................................................

2. ...........................................................
   ...........................................................

3. ...........................................................
   ...........................................................

Keeping this commitment is important to me because: ......................
...........................................................
...........................................................
...........................................................
...........................................................

..................................
*your signature*

Now, put the 2 parts of your MINI PLAN together!

I encourage you to rip out the next page and put it somewhere you can see it. Let it be your daily reminder to treat yourself with support and care and your daily commitment to yourself.

(you can also take a photo and keep it on your phone)

# MY REFUEL AND RECHARGE
## MINI PLAN

### 3 DAILY ANCHORS
### to fuel my energy

1. .....................................................
2. .....................................................
3. .....................................................

### 3 THINGS I WILL DO LESS
### to avoid draining my energy

1. .....................................................
2. .....................................................
3. .....................................................

# WRITE A NOTE-TO-SELF

NOTE TO SELF

Share your NOTE-TO-SELF on social media!

Tag @natalykogan
#awesomehuman

NOTE TO SELF

Maybe you're not
   unmotivated.

Maybe you're exhausted
and just need to fuel
your energy, REST, and
 be a kind friend to
      yourself.

@natalykogan

The most important thing I want
you to understand about motivation
is this:

Motivation is an outcome.

When you don't feel motivated,
it means that some of the
inputs into motivation are missing.

It doesn't mean that you're lazy.

Or that you should label yourself
"unmotivated."

It means that you need to
figure out which motivation
inputs are missing and focus
on them.

Here's a flowchart
I made for myself
one day, when I
couldn't find my
motivation

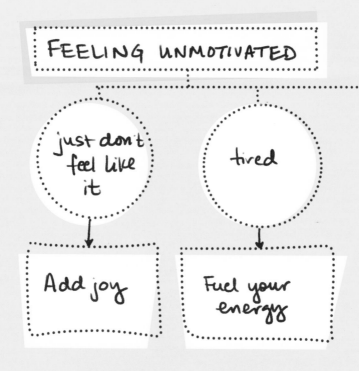

I've got an awesome
"add joy" practice for you next →

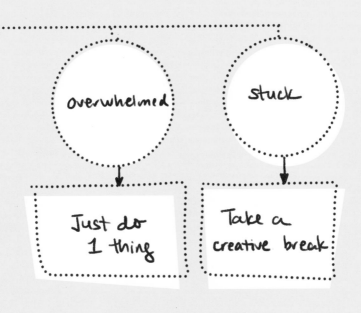

...and the others are
in this journal!

## Here's the "add joy" practice:

If you don't feel like doing something that you **need** to do, add something that you **want** to do.

This is called Temptation Bundling and it's an awesome way to add joy to fuel your motivation.

Here's how to do it:

### MINI NEUROSCIENCE LESSON

The human brain has a "present" bias — it prefers to settle for a smaller reward now than wait for a larger one in the future.

Temptation Bundling works because it makes activities with delayed benefits more instantly gratifying.

# CREATE YOUR TEMPTATION BUNDLE

**Step 1** — Choose an activity you need to do (but don't feel motivated to do or have trouble sticking to)

```
[                                    ]
```

need-to-do activity

**Step 2** — Choose an activity that brings you joy and that you want to do (and one that you could do at the same time as the need-to-do one)

```
[                                    ]
```

want-to-do activity

**Step 3** — Only do your want-to-do activity when you do your need-to-do one (this is very important — stay exclusive!)

```
[                                    ]
```

this is your temptation bundle

NOTE TO SELF

Spend less energy on
"How will they judge _me_?"
and more energy on
"How could I help _them_?"

@natalykogan

STRUGGLING WITH

SELF-DOUBT

( or feeling not good enough)

When you're doing something new or challenging - or thinking about doing something new or challenging - it's completely normal to feel self-doubt.

Your brain is worried about all the uncertainty and its fear turns into thoughts of doubt.

But you can give your brain something better to focus on:

your BIGGER WHY, which is all about how what you're doing helps others or contributes to something bigger than you.

# Practice shifting your attention from self-doubt to your Bigger Why

## Self-doubt

"I'm going to mess up during my presentation"

## Bigger Why

"What I share in my presentation can help people."

## MINI NEUROSCIENCE LESSON

Focusing on your values
and how what you do
helps others puts your
brain into a pro-social
mindset, which increases
motivation and improves
your confidence and
your performance.

If your brain keeps telling you
that you are "not good enough,"
here's what you need to do:

Step 1
Remember that your
brain doesn't report
facts but makes up stories.

Step 2
Remind yourself
that you don't need
to go along with your
brain's unhelpful stories

Step 3
EDIT the made-up
"not good enough" story.

(If you've practiced Editing Your Thoughts on p.25
this will be easier to do! So if you haven't
done that practice, now is a good time.)

# EDIT YOUR "NOT GOOD ENOUGH" STORY

Your "not good enough" story )

Is this story true?

| FACTS that support it | FACTS that counter it |
| --- | --- |
|  |  |

Remember: What you think someone else thinks is **not** a fact.

Once you're done, look at the columns:

Which one has more facts in it?

I've done this practice with hundreds of people and have never seen anyone have more facts in the first column.

The human brain really loves to make up stories.

So the next time your brain tells you another "not good enough" story, come back here and <u>EDIT IT!</u>

NOTE TO SELF

Instead of wasting
your energy wondering
how you will get
it all done,
Start doing.

@natalykogan

FEELING

OVERWHELMED

( with too much to do
  or too much going on )

When you have a lot to do or think about, your brain can get overwhelmed.

So the best way to help your brain is to...

... ZOOM IN on the next step you can take, the 1 thing you can do right now.

## JUST DO 1 THING

**Step 1** : Choose 1 thing you need
to get done and can do now

**Step 2** : Write it down

**Step 3** : GO AND DO IT!

\* Do not do anything else. \*

Oh, except for this

Put your phone face down right here

DO NOT
_____

pick it up

until you have

done your 1 thing.

**Step 4:** When you have finished doing your 1 thing, go back and cross it out.

IDEA Next time, you can write your 1 thing on a Post-it Note or a piece of paper and then cross it out or rip it up when you are finished.

## MINI NEUROSCIENCE LESSON

Your brain loves a sense of progress. Every time you accomplish something, however small, your brain releases dopamine, which gives you a sense of satisfaction and motivates you to keep going toward your goal and accomplish more things.

(OK, you can go get your phone now...)

## NOTE TO SELF

When you take care
of _yourself_,
you take care of every
_other_ _self_ you impact.

@natalykogan

STUCK IN THE

"SELF-CARE IS SELFISH"

LOOP

(and feel guilty about

taking time for myself)

If your brain makes you feel guilty about taking care of yourself, you are not alone. My brain did this all the time...

...until neglecting myself led to my burnout.

That's when I learned a huge lesson:

YOU CAN'T GIVE

WHAT YOU DON'T HAVE

The only way you can give to others is if you have enough emotional, mental, and physical energy...

...which you get by practicing self-care.

I want to introduce you
to a concept that
helped me break through
my self-care guilt.

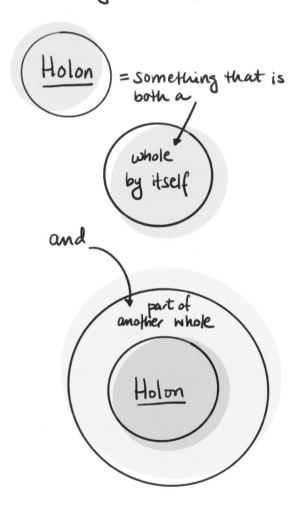

Holon = something that is
both a

whole
by itself

and

part of
another whole

Holon

For example, a bicycle wheel is a HOLON.

It is a whole by itself

and a part of a bicycle ...
... without which the bicycle can't function.

# YOU ARE A HOLON!

You are a "whole"
and an essential part of
other wholes in your life...

...and you can only positively
contribute to them if you
have enough energy.

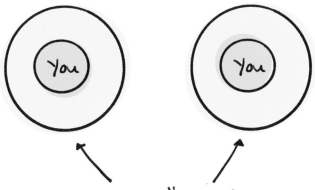

What other "wholes"
are you part of?

( group of friends, team, relationship, etc.)

Pick 1 "whole" in which you are a HOLON, and get specific about how your practice of self-care positively impacts it.

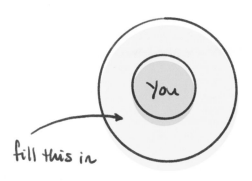

You

fill this in

When I practice self-care:

································································
································································
································································
································································
································································
································································
································································
································································
································································

This is your Bigger Why for making your self-care a priority.

Do this for another "whole"
in which you are a Holon.

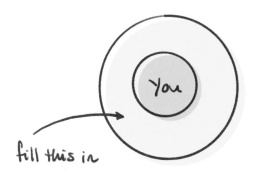

fill this in

When I practice self-care:

........................................................
........................................................
........................................................
........................................................
........................................................
........................................................
........................................................
........................................................
........................................................

This is your Bigger Why for
making your self-care a priority.

Dear Awesome Human,

Thank you.

Thank you for making me and this journal part of your journey.

Thank you for choosing to create a more supportive relationship with yourself.

Thank you for courageously practicing some things that were challenging.

Thank you for being.

And for being an Awesome Human.

Now, go and make yourself your very own Awesome Human Award — you've earned it!

With love and gratitude,

Nataly, your fellow Awesome Human

P.S. I would LOVE to hear from you! My email is nataly@happier.com and yes, I read all the emails myself!

AWESOME HUMAN

.........................................
your name

You are an Awesome Human
because:

AWARD

# ABOUT THE AUTHOR

A leading expert on emotional fitness, Nataly Kogan is an entrepreneur, best-selling author, and keynote speaker on a mission to help millions of people embrace their Awesome Human, struggle less, and thrive more in work and life!

Nataly immigrated to the US as a refugee from the former Soviet Union when she was 13 years old. Starting her American life in the projects and on welfare, she learned English by watching *Who's the Boss?* on repeat.

She went on to reach the highest levels of success as a technology and finance executive and entrepreneur. But after years of chasing a nonexistent state of nirvana, Nataly suffered a debilitating burnout that led her to find a new way to live and work.

Today, she helps Awesome Humans break free from daily burnout, unleash their full human potential, and experience more joy and meaning by sharing her unboring, science-backed Happier Method™—and her signature positive energy!

Nataly is a sought-after international keynote speaker and has appeared in hundreds of media outlets, including the *Wall Street Journal, Harvard Business Review,* the *New York Times,* TEDx Boston, and SXSW. She is the founder of Happier, Inc., and has worked with hundreds of top companies, teams, and leaders through her Happier @ Work and leadership programs.

Nataly is the author of *Happier Now*, *Gratitude Daily*, and *The Awesome Human Project* and hosts *The Awesome Human Podcast*, which people call their "best-self hour."

Nataly began painting when she turned 40 and is a self-taught abstract artist. She loves bright colors, overuses the word "awesome," and is the funniest person in her family. (Just ask her husband and daughter, her favorite Awesome Humans.)

Please visit natalykogan.com to invite Nataly to speak to your organization, sign up for her awesome weekly emails, and get fueled by tons of resources for Awesome Humans, including videos, art, and more!

# ABOUT SOUNDS TRUE

Sounds True is a multimedia publisher whose mission is to inspire and support personal transformation and spiritual awakening. Founded in 1985 and located in Boulder, Colorado, we work with many of the leading spiritual teachers, thinkers, healers, and visionary artists of our time. We strive with every title to preserve the essential "living wisdom" of the author or artist. It is our goal to create products that not only provide information to a reader or listener but also embody the quality of a wisdom transmission.

For those seeking genuine transformation, Sounds True is your trusted partner. At SoundsTrue.com you will find a wealth of free resources to support your journey, including exclusive weekly audio interviews, free downloads, interactive learning tools, and other special savings on all our titles.

To learn more, please visit SoundsTrue.com/freegifts or call us toll-free at 800.333.9185.

sounds true
WAKING UP THE WORLD